VERSE

I0149698

by
MIRIKA MAYO
CORNELIUS

VERSE

VERSE

VERSE

This is a work of fiction and poetry. Names, characters, places and incidents are either products of the author's imagination or are used fictitiously. Any resemblance to actual events or locales or persons, living or dead, is entirely coincidental.

An Akirim Press Publishing
Book Cover by Mirika Mayo Cornelius/Akirim Press
www.akirimpress.com

Flower photo credit: beautiful bloom blooming blossom 133472 from Pexels by Anthony royalty-free download

VERSE

VERSE

DEDICATION

to my son

May no one quiet you from speaking the truth because in truth there is freedom.

The truth will make you free. – Jesus

VERSE

VERSE

TABLE OF CONTENTS

VERSE

VERSE

VERSE

VERSE

VERSE

VERSE

BLACK-OWNED

Sprawled out with melanated bronze
and dusted with blackened coal,
tainted with ivory coffee
and flavored with molten gold.

Sprinkled with dark sesame
and washed in midnight tea,
doused with pleasant pepper,
and priceless like mahogany.

Drank as midnight dew
from charred glasses of steel,
tucked in shades of mushrooms,
and rooted in universal zeal.

Chocked full of burned shimmer
and rocked in majestic tone,
dripping with cinnamon and cocoa,
my skin is black-owned.

Splattered like a mocha sundae,
and stretched with caramel wood,
complete with copper veins,
and spread like generations should.

Created like the sun struck sky,

VERSE

breathtaking like the tawny breeze,
delivering like the sound of brass trumpets,
and stronger than cedar trees.

Blatant as the blinding forests
and cunning like the black fox,
explosive like earth's center
and as lengthy as black locs.

Cool like black jade
and hot as black jet stone,
as timeless as the black hole,
my skin is black-owned.

Gentle like sable velvet
and sharp like black flint,
bronze like Jesus's feet
and soothing like dark mint.

Bitter like pitch licorice
and sweet like innocent's rage,
flowing likc oil's fountain
blanketing the world stage.

Endless like diamond mines
and swift like black doves,
marked like inked lead
and bold like black love.

Bonded by genes

cloaked from the Throne,
gifted in majestic mercies,
my skin is black-owned.

WHO'S SHE?

Who's she over there looking at me?
Eyeing me down, taking her notes.
If she struts my way,
I'll shove it down her throat.
Make her eat the garbage she wrote
about me,
cried about me,
as she called the cops and lied on me.

Who's he over there staring at us?
He better come get her.
I don't wanna have to hit her.
I don't mind a fight
just like I don't mind a fuss.
If she keeps coming my way,
her body will hit that dust.

Who's she gawkin' at?
Is it the color of my skin

that has her so bent?
Is it the clothes I'm wearing
or the money I spent?
She thinks I stole it.
Yeah, I know I'm right.
She just better not walk this way
and put her hands on me
because I'm laying her out tonight.

THE SUFFOCATION

No matter how much I try to hold my head up high,
I'm suffocating.

At first, it seemed I could cope.
If I could just make it to another breath,
if my muscles would just stretch.
Life shouldn't be this hard,
and all this pain I shouldn't have to disregard.
I just want to live.
Instead, I'm suffocating.

There is food in my fridge,
but it will be empty tomorrow.
There isn't much that can ease this sort of sorrow
because everyone sees me with a roof over my head
and clothes on my back,

VERSE

and even with all this,
I put on this fake smile like I'm living the dream...
when I'm really dreaming.
I'm dreaming of when my days
won't be filled with so much rain
and my nights won't be filled with so much sunshine.
I can't go out without an umbrella.
I can't even go to sleep without staying awake,
worrying about what's at stake.
I'm suffocating.

My children sleep in the same bed at night,
tucked in tight, as I lean against their door
so the sound of their breathing can soothe me.
At least they are alive and well
with so many ideas to show and tell...
while I'm ashamed of my stories,
dreams and ignorant lullabies
that I used to convince myself of year after year.
I would believe I could do anything,
pull myself out of anywhere.
I'm suffocating.

Too afraid to ask anyone for help
because of the way I know they will spread
my situation into the streets, the sweltering heat...
it makes it nearly impossible to not accept defeat.
I want to say I need a couple more dollars to make
ends meet, when the truth is I need a couple hundred
of those dollars before they cast me and my family
out.
That's what will happen without a doubt.

VERSE

Then what? I work!
But I'm suffocating.

Tomorrow something might pull through for me.
Until then, I will hold my head up high and work until
there is no more work left in me.
I just don't want to die...
Because I'm suffocating.

BLACK SHEEP

Don't you worry, Black Sheep.
Here's what you do.
Let them stalk, talk and marvel
all over you.
Let them giggle, wiggle and
make fun of your wool.
Let them mock you, Black Sheep,
You ain't the fool.

Don't you worry, Black Sheep.
Here's what you do.
Prance, dance and move
all those evil words away from you.
Hold your head up so high
that the birds perch on your tip,
Sway your body side to side,
Be proud of your misfit.

VERSE

Don't you worry, Black Sheep.
Here's what you say.
Sing over all their songs,
and merry over their silly ways.
Whisper over their murmurs
and scream over their shouts.
Their voices amount to nothing.
They don't know what you're about.

Don't you worry, Black Sheep.
Here is what you pray.
Say Lord, dear Lord,
thank you for making me this way.
Thank you for making my hair kinky
and not down my back straight,
and for the color of my wool,
Lord, that black is great.
It cuddles me when I'm cold,
and it hides me in the dark.
It reminds me of how they hurt You
so like You, King, I'm set apart.

YESTERDAY

Yesterday, I watched somebody die.
draped inside dark brown linen and caressed in warm
air, drifted into the cold, where no mercy dwells
and no sadness dispels.

Yesterday, I watched Death come.

Had an axe in one hand and pain in the other,
ready to chop through Joy
to depress our sisters and brothers.

Yesterday, I watched him kill that little boy,
Got it all on tape,
used it to try and shut my mouth,
paying out stacks upon stacks,
Like all those numbers will bring that innocent boy
back.

Yesterday, I watched them all die.
Heard the chatter of why they had to
"pull the triggers on the n*ggers."
Words never been so mean and continuous,
some still remained oblivious,
to the death that involves them all,
as one body, two bodies, three bodies fall.

Yesterday, I watched somebody die.
Today, I cry.

DON'T FORGET, CHILDREN

I'm gonna write this down so it won't be forgotten.

VERSE

I'm gonna do like GOD did and write it in stone,
then teach it to my children until it feeds their bones.
They will read it and rehearse because it should be
memorized. It will penetrate their pores whether they
be deaf, dumb or blind.

That's what I'm gonna do for my kids.

I'm gonna make them draw it every morning
and then rip it up every night so that they know how to
keep it tucked away inside and hold on to it tight,
that precious thing that one day might be out of sight.

I'm gonna teach my babies something that I know for
myself,
that He was with me through my good and bad times,
even those days when I didn't have a dime,
and the tax man had no mercy on me, even though I
was trying.
It was Jesus Who hung with me, just so I could make
it through, and, to my kids I'll say, He'll do the same
for you.

I'm gonna teach my offspring the River of Life, the
Lion of
Judah and how He paid the price.
I'm gonna teach them so they will never be fooled,
want to follow the wrong way or break the rules.
I want them to know that Jesus loves them on good
and bad days, and no matter what the cost, they'll live
with Him worry free one day.

A FOREFATHERS' DISGRACE

For my descendants,
I stripped my skin on trees,
ripped my mouth on thorns,
stabbed rocks with fractured knees,
spit up guts of blood and mourned,
kept vision when I wanted to go blind,
just jug my own self hard in both my eyes.
I didn't want to see the day they took you away,
but now I need to say, you've left me.
You chose to betray.

You won't remember me anymore,
talkin' 'bout *how y'all not like us*,
shoutin' *how y'all tough as nails*,
but ain't one soul of y'all livin' free today
been drug through our kinds of hells.
Listenin' to you talk big and yell bad,
like you would've survived my plight,
but on this racist land, with or without good limbs,
I still had to fight.

Been raped near 'bout thirty times,
by thirty different white men.
Done watched my daddies hung and burned

23

in my face over and over again.
Near 'bout lost my mind to my hells,
Heaven knows, I think I did.
But I had just enough fight left over to
wean by baby kin
'fore they was snatched from me, all alone,
enough time for me to carve the word
SURVIVE in their bones.

I remember when I used to be your queen.
I remember when I used to be your king.
Kidnapped, but head held high.
Sold, but taught you never to die.
Strangled, but still taught you to read.
Muffled, but still taught you to breathe…FREEDOM.
But now that I'm all gone,
and the dirt has bruised my black face,
you treat me like a disgrace,
my memory you want to erase.
Hear you shoutin' from the rooftops that you're tired
of
hearin' 'bout me and the history we share.
I never thought that one day
you wouldn't care.

And to think you became free off of a bloody,
enslaved and still deadly proud Black me.

JET BLACK SHE

As soon as she entered outside, she knew it.
She tiptoed on the pavement, and she blew it.
Every face raised and saw her noise out loud.
She shrank from the crowd.
They dropped their faces back into secluded spaces.
She found another way out.
She knew what it was about.

As soon as she exited inside, she knew it.
She was overlooked and mistook by many
who only saw her as good, but for only one thing.
Her intelligence was hampered,
Her brilliance, tampered.
Everyone thought they were better
than jet black she.

As soon as her reflection was seen,
others grew mean.
Her words were elegant,
spoken languages unknown.
Her phrases, bold.
She never had a tongue slip,
but she was awarded a hard slap;
the bruise only showing up as a light tap.
Her pain unaware.
Her burdens only she had to bear.

They all thought they were better than she.

Her jet black skin.
Jet black me.

BORN INTO SLAVERY

Just yesterday, I would have been born into slavery. I
would have had the skin beat from my back because
I'm black.
I would have had the children raped out of me because
I wasn't free.

Just yesterday, I would have grieved my toiling
mothers enough to remember their names over my
own.
I would have groaned in the heartbreak of my father
who never had a chance to be the man that he wouldn't
disown.

Just yesterday, I would have been born with white
people shouting at me, making it rain down dollars
while they opened my legs to look and bid.
I would have been dragged off the stage, thrown into a
cage, so even more white babies could learn how to
mistreat me.

Just yesterday, I would have never known a good
memory because happiness would have become my
enemy.

VERSE

I would have clung to sadness for just a spell until that sadness turned into the rage that sent all those white people to hell.

Just yesterday, I would have been born into slavery. I would have had to patch the skin back onto my back with a stranger's hand.
I would have had to layer the floor with the blood of my masters and painted my face with their veins…and felt no shame.

Just yesterday, I would have had to wander through the wilderness, trained to search and sneak.
Finally, I would have found my freedom and secured my future descendant's peaceful sleep.

THE SEDUCTION

Guide me through the perfect time on earth,
when the Garden of Eden had no dirt birth and had no ribbed side.
Kick me into that dimension where
I wouldn't have to hide behind banana leaves and cradle
myself beneath flowing waves of water because my black body would make even the sun feel less stunning because I'm so hot.

VERSE

Pour me out like the flood so I can cleanse
what contaminates my paradise and soak what
degrades it
until it alters its perception, deciding on a
new perfect conception. I would regrow the trees and
calm the breeze, redefining my caves, shaping the
storm
into a failing hurricane.

Weave me through the perfect time on earth,
when woman met man and there was no murder
amongst the child and no envy striking the brow.
We wouldn't have to rush our way from death nor
immerse ourselves in life because we would be

the only seduction.

SHORT NAILS, SKINNY THIGHS

I grew up like a stalk in the deep, deep sunshine,
flicked my feet in the puddles of muddy waters and
held on tight to my chair as my mother hot combed my
kinky hair.
It was all there.

VERSE

From the time I spent my first dime, caught some Jumping Jacks and committed my first crime...yep, I had these short nails and skinny thighs.

I tried once or twice to put on some crafts, make my fingers laugh and have a good time, change my destiny by altering my look, just like taking on a new story instead of writing my own book, but those long, lovely things made me feel so out of place because no matter how much I tried to embrace... them... they just didn't work for me...
write for me...
type for me...
live for where I was going and wanted to be. So I left them there. Broke them suckers all off my fingers without a care, and I finally felt free to be me, once again with my short nails and skinny thighs.

Some older people would stare me up from my long, lingering toes to the top of my dome, and they would tell at me, just yell at me, that I needed to go back home and get some meat on my bones. It was just about to slide off the side of my mind how they could stand to run a few miles from time to time instead of sitting their tired tails on the fronts of their porches smokin' torches and chewing hay, but I let them speak anyway, and I also let them laugh, stare, shake their heads and sigh.

Did I feel like making time to cry? Maybe so, but my Mama didn't raise no chump, you know? Crying never

came easy for a girl my size...yeah, even with short
nails and skinny thighs.

I came out of my Mama's womb not a moment too
soon. I didn't know a thing, not even my names - my
first from my last or my middle - it all sounded the
same. But what I soon unmasked or better yet
unearthed, wasn't by chance but by my awakening in
The Rebirth - that I didn't need the greed that would
attempt to make me beg and plead to be accepted by
anything or anyone who thought they were the only
bright and brand new thing created under the sun.
Like they were more special than I ... just because they
had long nails and plump thighs.
My, my. What a lie.

CONDITIONING

I don't want to lose myself. I don't want to lose
anything about me, just because of all the mockery.
I love the way my neck grows as far up from my
shoulders as it possibly can grow, and I adore the way
my lips form succulent pillows. Everything about me
is long enough and big enough, smooth enough and
even wrinkled enough.

The mole on the side of my left eye reminds me of my
ancestry that can go back for many, many moons. As
a matter of fact, if it ever went away, it would be way

VERSE

too soon because if every picture burned up in flames and every moment became lost in my memory, my children would still be able to find me based off of those intricate and minute things that make me seem so laughable, like I'm such an anomaly. Like I'm so funny...to look at.

So no, I don't want any conditioning.

My hair curls around my shoulders like it's tickled pink. It won't relax for anything, and I, honestly, really don't want it to stand down or lay down to a system of laws that would only assume it can force it to become something that it's not. At the root of the whole journey, when the water flows through it...or when I flow through the water... it's still coming back. It never went anywhere, defying each and every single odd that would dare shut it down. I earned my crown.

Conditioning...no. It's not my thing.

Why would I embrace something so blinding, as if I need to counteract the facts that make me attract all the attention, be it bad or good. Hell… you need to see me… and enjoy all this versatility, just like I need to see everything about your make up that's not made up.

It's only a matter of time before we all disappear, and if we're not careful, no one will ever know that we were truly here.

Conditioning.

THAT BLACK

The so-called good black,
the kind the massahs like,
The kind of brown skin that lies down
without a fight,
The kind of black skin that doesn't snap
back, clap back or straighten you out.
Massahs know what that black is about.

The good black don't stir up no trouble,
tip toes around the cracks and rolls with no rumble,
catches the words of massah's lips like they are
diamonds and pearls,
carries their superior missions all around the world.

Then there's the so-called bad black,
The kind of black that massahs despise.
The kind that flicks their eyes and twists their necks,
won't bless ole massah's land because they didn't
burn it to the ground yet.

That bad black doesn't let anything slide,
won't give massah anywhere to hide,
won't help him run, won't shade him from the burning
sun.

VERSE

A white massah he came, but a bruised one he will
become.

That black…
the one that hits back,
the one that sits where she desires
and if you try and move her, she'll set your
soul on fire.
If massah raises a hand at him,
he'll meet it high up in the air,
lift massah from the ground by his throat
and let him die there.
No need for a tree, and no need for a crowd.
He'll shake the life from him and
drop him to the ground.

It's that black, the kind that doesn't yield,
the kind that might have picked that cotton
but also poisoned the field,
the kind that chooses to never die
but live.

FOOLED

Gave you my body,
but it wasn't free.
It meant nothing for you,
but everything to me.

VERSE

My ears burned with hope
as you spoke to them with tenor
notes on a chord,
laying on me, training me,
like this was how it was supposed to be.

Had me thinking that I was something,
something more than what you craved for,
but more like that something you'd die for.
That's what I felt you thought of me,
that I was more than just some … body.

I was rich when your eyes met mine
for the very first time,
the second time richer,
and the third time, the richest woman alive.
Tossed everything I had away,
just so I could spend every dime I had with you,
run around, let loose until our time was through.
It was just me and you.

From the moment we held hands
it was never just a latch of luck in our
fingers' strands, the locks of love
in each moment our fingers met and our palms
massaged.
Had me believing we were a match under God.

Then, all those hopes died.
How you hurt me so bad and sat our love aside.
You lied.

VERSE

It was in my hopes I fell for you,
but the real you was so untrue.
How I wish I'd never fallen in love with
an imagined you.

JESUS

Innocent He came, and Innocent he went.
Never hid a dollar and never stole a cent.
Threw Him to the masses and thought He would burn.
Like a slave, they hung Him high, but He will return.

Soft He stomped and flowers bloomed beneath His feet.
Anywhere He looked, the people filled in the streets.
Some slapped Him with curses and mocked Him with thorns,
Like a slave, they beat Him, but they will reap their reward.

Like a blanket, He warmed, and like a siren, He warned
People not believing, blind though plainly seeing.
Some ran into each other, some fell into the creek,
Like to a slave, they shut their ears to Him so they couldn't hear him speak.

Like thunder, He sounded, and like lightening, He struck.

VERSE

Trumpets blew out flames as an orchestra sang His
Name.
Some tried to run, and some shook the ground.
Like a slave, He served, but now He wears His crown.

GENETIC MEMORY

I've never been kidnapped,
but somehow I know how it feels.
I've never forgotten,
but somehow I lost that way.
I've never been terrified,
but somehow, it's what my conscience
reminds me of.
I've never been enslaved,
but somehow I was.

I've never been royal,
but somehow I know how it feels.
I've never remembered,
but somehow I know how to do it.
I've never been happy,
but somehow a smile bends my skin.
I've never won,
but somehow, I win.

I've never been raped,

but somehow the pain taps me.
I've never been alone,
but somehow I find myself there.
I've never been sad,
but yesterday I cried at a joke.
I've never been whipped,
but my skin still broke.

I've never been without my mother,
but I've missed her for thousands of years.
I've never been without my father,
but I wonder about him through my tears.
I've always had siblings,
but never seen them a day on this earth.
I've seen plenty deaths,
but somehow missed many births.

I've never been arrested,
but I can't free my wrists.
I've never spoken softly,
but my words are dismissed.
I've never drank from an empty glass,
but I have taken down hot air.
I've never touched hatred's body,
but I know it's still there.

JAIL DECREE

VERSE

I'll sit in my jail,
in my cell with four walls,
listen to the nighttime
hammer out freedom calls,
those same freedom calls
that I misunderstand
because I've never left
these cell bars to walk on
free land.

I've been in here since
I can remember,
and that's not too far back.
I was only eight years old
when they put a shoe on my back
and told me my mother
would never see me again,
so young to become a loser,
and too young to win.

Now I'm fifteen and still
treated like a grown man,
sitting inside this cement,
praying it spits me green land,
That wasn't a plan,
so I thought to take my life,
but what an imbalanced sacrifice.
Even though I was put here
'cause of someone else's crime…

I won't let them steal my rhyme
or my rhythm,

won't let them kill my spirit
in this filthy prison.
They toss me to and fro and scrub
the floors with my black skin
because no one, not no one,
can see the hell I'm in.

Only God alone,
He is my Strength.
He will atone,
and that last lie I saw part from your lips,
forcing that chain across my
back like a whip,
you will one day feel worse than that
at His Throne.
You will be judged for what you did to me,
just you and you alone.

BLOODY RESURRECTION

Get the knife, and don't be scared.
Carve out words that you never said.
Slice the curves so that they drench in blood.

VERSE

Soak the walls and make it flood.

Saturate the cities, and then watch them drain.
Feel it all evaporate, condense and pour red rain.
Trace the mud puddles it creates from the dirt,
and then dip the knife in to break the earth.

Transfuse the death to bring the earth back to life.
Tremble the plates to make the lava run deep.
Set fire to the bones that went cold in the trees.
Cut through the graves. Now let them breathe.

REBELLION

When we ran, we did it fast.
When we slept, it wasn't real.
When we spoke, it was deception.
When we laughed, it was false perception.

When we failed, it was on purpose.
When we kneeled, it was to pray.
When we walked, it was to pave.
When we cooked, it was all we gave.

When we gave birth, it was to teach.
When we shouted, it was to preach.
When we understood, we really forgot.
When we remembered, it was all we got.

VERSE

When we decided, it was done.
When we slit, it was many throats.
When we shot, there was dread.
When we fled, they were all dead.

MERCILESS BRICKS

He was thrown onto one brick.
He was kicked onto another.
He was shot on the bottom brick.
He was my black little brother.

She was slapped onto one brick.
She was choked on another.
She was shot on the same bottom brick.
She died just like my brother.

They were shoved down on a brick.
They were screaming side by side.
They were shot begging for mercy.
They were left on the bricks to die.

REVERSED

What if roles were reversed
And the House was Black?
What if the whips pulled the skin
from the white man's back?

What if roles were reversed
And his-story wasn't his?
What if the children were taught
Black history and that smart whites weren't real?

What if roles were reversed
And the media was pro-Black?
What if when whites got innocently shot,
their childhood shenanigans they would attack?

What if roles were reversed
And Hollywood cast whites as maids?
What if whites were only shown as butlers,
thugs, and slaves?

What if the roles were reversed
And bad police officers got locked up?
What if the good officers spoke the truth aloud
to ease the hearts of an angry crowd?

What if the roles were reversed
And Blacks had all the cash?
What if white people had to start from the bottom
and Blacks shouted *life ain't fair, get your own stash*?

VERSE

What if the roles were reversed
And the poor dominated the rich?
What if they couldn't forgive the atrocities, sucked
you dry, shouted *work harder*,
and then beat you across the back with sticks?

What if the roles were reversed
And white skin was the sin?
What if whites were called
ugly and ignorant over and over again?

What if the roles were reversed
And the white blind man could finally see?
What if he called racists on all their racist stories
and asked that simple question,

Why did you lie about them to me?

DARE

I honestly don't care how you feel about this.
I just want to write.
I just want to tell it how it is
without your two cents and without your sensitivities
without your correctness and without your hypocrisies,
without your finger pointing at me like you're my
mother,

without your eyes bucking like I'm an other,
like I'm not human, like I'm not aware,
like I'm not worthy, like I'm not there,
like I'm sick, even ill in the head,
but no I'm not.
I'm just saying it like it should be said.
I'm not hate-filled nor am I a pretender,
not a rude elaborator
or a dismissive conjugator.
I cross every T and dot every I,
learned to think before I could speak or write,
and my mom is my alibi.
That's why I really don't care how you feel about this.
I really don't care.
You pushed me to it, just try to shut me up.
Dare.

DON'T ANSWER

They called her a thug.
When she batted the lashes from her
pretty brown eyes and
When she sat back and crossed her
rounded thighs and
When she lifted her pinky as she
placed down her drink and
When she leaned forward just enough

to make them all think.
They called her a thug.

They called him a thug.
When he was born from his
mother's womb and
When he became old, gray and his
body was ready for the tomb and
When he was just a boy with his
handsome walk and his confident talk and
When he stared them in their eyes and
his strong innocence they despised.
They called him a thug.

They called us thugs.
When we graduated from school and we
told our children to do the same and
When we refused to lose, limp or lay down and
become disabled no matter how shaky the ground and
When we survived even the poison that
was shot in our veins and
When we still remain and
call ourselves proudly by our birth names.

They call us thugs.

TO THE AFRICAN SLAVE TRADER

African Slave Trader, was it worth it, was it worth it, oh was it worth all of what you did when you broke the bowels of Africa open and sold all her kin?

African Slave Trader, was it worth it, was it worth it, oh was it worth all you set aflame, when you torched to ash the beauty of blackness before the world and tarnished its very name?

African Slave Trader, was it worth it, was it worth it, oh was it worth all you sowed in disgrace, believing wrongly that you found some monetary blessed grace for the Black lives you displaced?

African Slave Trader, was it worth it, was it worth it, oh was it worth all of the people you sold, not knowing those African people were the strength of your continent and worth far more than that worthless silver and gold?

African Slave Trader, was it worth it, was it worth it, oh was it worth all of the problems you caused, because even after 400 long years, Black people everywhere still live with those scars you and Europeans caused.

African Slave Trader, was it worth it?

TO THE EUROPEAN SLAVE TRADER

What? You think you're off the hook?
No. I just chose to check them first because
they signed off on the book.
But you, it was you who wrote the sequels,
all four-hundred years in,
shaving our heads, selling our kids,
and hanging our kin,
busting our wombs and boiling our skin.

You surrounded us with water,
and blinded us with trees,
took us by our wrists and
and shoved the mud up to our knees.
You claimed our rights and didn't pay your debts,
You took our money, burned our cities
until we had nothing left.

You changed the history books to make
yourselves look as brilliant as light.
You actually fooled yourselves
But God will make it right.
You toted the Bible and never quit,
never accurately interpreted the scriptures

VERSE

because you never intended to live by it.

What? You think you're still off the hook?
Forget your history, I'm writing this book.
You swore you were statuesque,
yeah, thought you were the head.
But now your own children are ashamed of you,
and your legacy is dead.

VERSE

BLACK LOVE'S NEW NATION

a short story in VERSE

With no memories of you,
I lend my imagination to create some,
partake in some of mental freedoms that were my
mother's mothers' venom and my father's fathers'
stifles because they never told me, wanted me survive
and never know the bullet of a white man's rifle.

I will remember us as children.
We would roll around in the high silky grasses, move
with the wind, and slither in the red sands, tricking the
birds overhead that we were food and not man.

Kind we were.

I will recall when it grew cool at night, so cool that we
would barricade ourselves in each other's arms to wait
on the sun's charm and the white bands to streak
across heaven's motherland.

One day, when we were four years old, we sneaked off
to watch the stars unfold, and we laughed when
everyone went crazy because we were nowhere
around.

VERSE

The old people claiming that a ghost came through and
led us both out when all we were doing was hiding,
picking wild berries from the bushes and hanging out.
It wasn't fun to watch everyone scold us when they
saw us stumbling back across the dung.
We stood back crying and watched as our parents got
the straps from where they hung.

When we were six years old, I will remember how we
would catch our older siblings making out behind the
palm oil trees. They would crouch down and cover
themselves behind the leaves. We would always get
them in trouble! You would run one way and I the
other.

By the time we were nine, we would practice the
cheek kiss all the time, and by the time we were
eleven, we would practice the tongue kiss over and
over again.
It was nasty the first time, and we laughed at each
other the second. The third and fourth kisses got better,
and by the fifth time, we were together.

At the thirteenth age, we both connected at the eyes
and joined at the heart.
By the time we were sixteen, there was something
powerful that wouldn't allow anything to tear us apart.
We both felt it, and it felt like hot rain, or maybe like
numb skin. It was very noticeable, outwardly and from
within.

VERSE

It was in our seventeenth year that we felt each other beyond the eyes of our spies.
We were both naked in the low lands and then on the plush hills.
We escaped and kept breaking through to our wills.
Our passions massaged each other, erotically intoxicating moans filled the sky, and the steam from our tenderness layered the atmosphere with an insane gentleness that made us go mad.
It was the highest form of intimacy we'd ever had.

As we made love atop of the peak of the mountain, causing the ice to melt and the sun to freeze, a rope wormed its way to the top, crawled around my waist and pulled us apart, dragging me from your arms, atop the boulders so sharp.
Africa's largest and meanest stabbed me in my back, as my body was hauled across the rocks, scream by scream, knock by knock.

Broken by my calls, my love chased after me, wounds and all, like an animal thirsting for the kill.
He tried to rescue me.
The last thing I saw was the blood streaming from his eyes, straining from every vein in his face.
He tried, but couldn't get to me because he would have died.

His swiftness wasn't swift enough, and his call wasn't loud enough, though every tree fell at its vibration.

VERSE

My body swept the mud, drawing a pathway between
villages and creating boundaries between life and
despair.
I was dragged so long and so far that eventually people
stopped looking and listening.
No one cared.

I remember taking one last look as they dragged me
across the earth by my neck, taking my ability to speak
or think ... no more oxygen to breathe until I forgot
where I was.
My mind in a blur as the ocean woke me up to bones,
crust, blood and pus.

I'd never been so close to another bare body before
that wasn't his.
I was naked and afraid to quiver, lost and resisting a
shiver.
Their sweat wasn't formed like ours, and their eyes
were large and lost, but like mine, our sight came with
a huge cost. Everywhere I turned was the sound of
metal on metal banging in my ears, but no matter
where I turned, my love was nowhere near.
I called him every day, but he never called me back by
my name, the name he would always call me – his –
because we were one in the same.

Until one day I forgot. As the noose tightened around
my veins, the harder it got to oxygenate my brain.
I choked until I nearly choked to death, and each time
I exhaled, my memories left. That's why I always tried
to hold my breath…five, four, three, two, one…

VERSE

I couldn't remember his voice, his smell or his sounds.
They were drowned out by all the shuffling around
they did with me and the strangers to whom I had
become attached.
My heart had been broken. I was never going back.

More voices began to stream into my ears, loud ones,
soft ones, and some that had no fear. Some only spoke
death and others spoke life.
My voice, an abrasive sound, never blended in with
the crowd.
Silence became my fence. I would hide my face inside
my breasts, clinging to the latest thumps that fought
against my chest.

Then, again, in one day, my belly started to push out.
A gift
when me and my love made miracles on that mountain
top, before they ripped our skin in half.
Day after day, I was bleeding, but then it came to a
halt.
The whole time, I wondered why that heavy flow had
stopped, thinking it was because of some disease I
caught from the white skin that tried to connect to
mine, to color the black off of me every night,
different ones, rockin' on the ocean, and all the time.
But when I landed and caught sight of what was
conceived, it was clear. My Black love was still here.

I saw him, and I kissed him all over again. His feet
looked like Africa's feet, and his hands like his
father's own, and when he kicked, I knew he was the

fastest, and when he cried, I knew he was the strongest
of them all.
His birthmark was set inside his back like his father's,
and his eyes were designed like mine, just like his
smile.
It was his time, and I couldn't let him die although I
wanted us to take up wings and fly.
He was my love's and mine.

I refused to teach him Africa in order to survive.
There was no need to put his life in danger, so I was
good to the pale stranger, the lashes going across my
heart instead of my body so my son wouldn't have to
see me bleed.
But soon, my heart ran cold, and I became bold.
My vessels became ice, and my mind became the
ocean with waves of methods to escape that ended up
drowning in the deepest parts.
Where we were, there was no end and also a lost start.

Believing my flesh of my flesh would soon come to
get us so we could flee,
I would imagine him as a cloud, hovering above me,
reaching down to save his baby, then his future
grandbabies, because they would keep coming out.
All would speak the new tongue better than me, but
then suddenly, being enslaved was taken to a whole
new degree when three white men snatched our son
from me.
Then, those cloud dreams of him rescuing his baby
faded away.

VERSE

I then knew we were here on this land to stay because there was no way I would choose to leave it without my only born baby.

Whispers were sent to me like the wind sends yellow dust leaping in the air, and the dust carried secret signs to me, letting me know my son was still alive, here or there.
He was big by now, and I was shrinking in size.
I never could hold myself up since his presence left my eyes.
The wood fence was so tall and the river so wide, I couldn't climb up, and I couldn't swim to the other side.

So, in the middle of the night, I would fill my hands with yellow dust, walk to the edge of the fence and give a light puff.
I knew that God, the One Who came to me in my darkest place, promising He would make it good and the evil He would erase.
I knew that He, my brand new Friend, would see my son through this harsh journey again and again,
and in my puff of yellow dust, He would send my kiss against my son's face, creating a mark that could forever be traced.

Back to me, he would come, and God didn't lie. I forever praised Him constantly, even when others would deny.
God sent him back to me in the twinkling of my eyes.
What felt like a long time, was made up in a minute.

VERSE

I hugged him and hugged him, for he was a grown man,
my New World descendant.
My son was tall and strong, and his face was clean as gold, but before I could finish touching his face, he looked beyond me down the slave auction road.

I turned to see that someone was calling me, just hollering my name, except my birth name had already been changed.
My son suddenly moved in front of me, because the person calling seemed deranged, like he was lost, even crazed.
His arms flailed high, and his limp ran slow,
but it was the voice that called me that shook me to my soul.
It was the same voice, same call, but several more years old.

He said he'd gotten caught on purpose and all on his own.
Said he promised he would find me and wouldn't ever leave me alone.
Told me he'd seen the ship, and it was to that same ship he'd volunteered. Said the same man he saw take me onboard the ship was glad to chain him in.
Said the European man laughed while the African man joked.
They exchanged him for weapons and threw him on the boat.

VERSE

Though he was in pain, he explained it was the happiest he'd been since.
Said he weighed the options, and he'd rather die than from me keep the distance.
He'd rather swim the oceans and drown, leave the earth and drop back down, just to hold me again, face to face, no matter if it was in a whole different place.

As he spoke through my son's large stature who was willing to protect me with his entire life, I gently touched my son's wrist, and he backed away twice.
Staring down at me with a loving heart, he knew something was different, that this man wasn't here to tear us apart.

My son stood there and watched something he'd never seen before in his life.
It was love … love … love… the greatest love as my love held me with all his might.
Unsure of what to do or even what to make of this man, he finally took a step forward, reached over and snatched back this strange man's hand.

"Who are you?" were the words that left his lips with fire,
but the new man to the land dipped his head and admired.
Immediately, he knew the young man who stood before him.
Yes, he knew him so well.

VERSE

It was the son he'd seen in the moon when it shined,
and he'd watched him grow up as he peered through
time.

"This man," I sang with tears on my face, "This one
right here promised to not leave me in disgrace.
This one right here was with me decades ago,
in a land that was brutal to me in the end, a land that
you don't know.
He risked his life and didn't know what was left to be
found…"

"But I had to go search. I knew my feet had to leave
familiar ground.
I had to ride the water and learn the sounds.
At first it was hard, but then it became clear.
I followed the sounds of your hearts. Just to find you, I
gave up everything to be here."

Then, all but too fast, panic struck, and we ran off
behind the trees.
We remained there, untamed there, in the noisy breeze.
We were concealed, never revealed, to all the white
people who were hunting runaway seed.
We had to try to escape from there because bondage
covered the entire land indeed.
For people like us, life was hunted to be split apart.
Love was always short and sweet before it became
bitter and tart.

My son went to my love, finally unguarded and well
aware

that it was his blood father standing there.
Before it was time to run further and maybe eventually die,
he embraced his father, and all they did was cry.
The cry was the purest rumble the earth had ever felt.
It was so pure that it made the hatred melt.
Just for a short spell, all was well,
but then we heard the dogs yell.

Suddenly, my love reached for me, pulled me in.
He touched me like he hadn't in a long time, over and over again.
Then, in that same moment, he shoved me away and moved our son, shouted for us to *run*!
Without a plan, I grabbed his hand to pull him on with us, but he put up a strong, horrible fuss before one of the dogs caught hold to us.
My son, in all his rage, all the furor he'd had to hold onto for all his natural born days, grabbed the mut like it was a flimsy stick, striking it to the ground until he killed it.

His father had never seen an anger so flared.
He moved to tell him *that's enough*, but immediately drew back nearly scared.
My son glared at him like he was a beast, like his father was something else for him to tread.
I jumped in between my son and him, as the dog lay there dead, shouting,
 "Don't fault him for not understanding you, baby,
because the rope hasn't yet lifted his head,
the dogs hadn't yet torn his flesh,

the salt hasn't burned inside his gashes,
their laughter hasn't silenced his happiness,
and his back still isn't paved with lashes.
He just got here and doesn't know what we had to
endure.
His way is still new, and he don't know what to do."

"So run, Mama! Run, and I'll fight. I'll fight these
white boys to death tonight. And you, you can go on,
too. I've been here this long alone. You can't tell me
what to do."
His anger was worse than a four legged beast, and his
mouth buckled like he was ready to feast.

My love stood up to him, moving me aside, telling
him,
"I'm here now, son, as your father, but I know now,
you must be my guide. I'm not here to leave you, but
if I have to, it will be by death. I won't let another
thing hurt you or your mama, so you go on, I will fight
until there is nothing of me left. Share your anger with
me, let me drink it down. Let me use it all up until me
and those white men are all in the ground. Share your
wisdom with me, on how they operate over here, so
just in case I live, I won't have anything to fear."

"There's no way, not one way, father, you can beat
them by yourself. They talk. They don't listen. They
shoot. They don't run. They smile before they kill, and
they gloat when they're done. Before they get you,
they will talk to calm you down, but if they try to grab
you, let 'em, then you wrestle them to the ground. If

there's more than one, get the gun, so know where
they stand. Pull the trigger quick, just know where the
bullet lands."

My love looked back at me and told me that I would
have to go, but like my son already knew, my love still
did not know.
He did not know that I wouldn't let my son fight
alone.
We were all warriors over here, Black bone of Black
bone.
I stood against my love, growing nearly to his size,
he knew I wasn't going anywhere.
I would fight with my son, side by side.

Two more dogs came, and as they leaped up high, with
both their fists, like twins, they knocked them from the
sky.
They stomped the lives from the four-footed beasts
and then saw the men who watched their muts fall
deceased.
It was their turn, so they were about to find out how
we would end this whole chase right now.

There were two white slave catchers and one Black. It
was that Black one we first glared at before turning
our attention back. I started my screaming, pretending
I was so frail.
I buckled. I fell. I even wailed.
My son knew I was puttin' on, but my love thought I
was being real. He didn't know the woman I'd
become, so different from what was in his head. I

VERSE

wasn't as weak as my appearance, and I wasn't no
stranger to choking a man dead.
My hands had become brutal, though soft as the cotton
I'd picked. My back had become strong, standing like
bricks against any fist or kick.

A gun was raised, and I reached behind.
My son leaped forward, but my love shoved him aside.
A gun went off, then I drew my knife, and when the
bullet didn't suffice, I cut the trigger man one huge
slice.
Blood poured as a rope pulled at my neck.
It tightened, I fell, and it rolled me two and fro.
Finally, I slit through the rope, and it had to let go.
Checking on my son who broke one white man's
bones against a tree, the Black man with his no good
rope stood there trembling at me.
He knew what he'd done, and he was worse than any
white slave catcher around.
I eyed his cut rope, and he guiltily put it down.
He walked over to the white man, who had my love on
the grass. The white slave catcher felt relieved until
the Black slave catcher beat his ass.

With an injured foot and two free hands, my love
stripped that white slave catcher of his gun and put a
bullet in his head.
Then, he leaned over to help the Black man from the
dirt,
but my son stormed over to his father, took the gun
and shot a bullet through the Black man's shirt.

VERSE

His father stumbled back, amazed at what he'd seen.
My son tucked the gun in his waist.
"He wasn't on our team. He would have run with us
for a while but then fell back to go tell.
He will do anything for *himself*, not to make sure *all* of
us are well."

I clung to my son, a proud mom that day.
My son was our son, but from now on, he would lead
the way.
My Black American child, oh African American child,
Nothing will hinder your way.
Let nothing or nobody hold you down.
Lead. You're here to stay.

SEED

They picked me.
They tossed me in with all the rest.
They shook me.
They dumped me and bruised my tender breasts.

They hosed me.
They dropped me.
They suffocated me 'til I couldn't see.
I couldn't move.
I couldn't breathe.
They wouldn't let me be.

VERSE

They walked all over me.
They stomped me.
They urinated on me, too.
They made me like the soot.
They stuck me like glue.

They soaked me.
They poked me.
They drowned me in the mud.
They thought I'd died.
They thought I failed.
I held my breath and didn't wail.

I fought back.
I broke through.
I woke up.
I stayed woke, too.
I swallowed the fear.
I broke through the shell.
I learned to breathe through the mud.
I escaped from hell.

The light saw me.
That was enough.
Where they thought they buried me,
God raised me up.

MISTY BRUISED EYES

VERSE

Crying never solved a thing.
Screaming solved another.
Shouting removed the crowd,
followed by a beating like no other.

Smiling never solved a thing.
Silence hid the surprise.
Whispering removed the shame
of my misty bruised eyes.

CROWNED BLACK

He spoke to me crazy,
and I laughed in his face.
Even though he thought it was,
nothing he said was full of grace.
He checked me out,
from my hair to my skin,
but then
I nearly choked on his words,
as a matter of fact, I did.

He said I was fine,
and as sharp as a tack.
He stood there amazed,
saying I was too beautiful to be black.

I stepped back from his lane

and created my own,
looked him in his face,
told him to leave me alone.

He jumped back, angry,
as I cocked back my head.
"All Black people are beautiful, and
to hell with what you just said."

ENVY

We clashed.
She bashed.
We spoke.
She choked.
I advised.
She ignored.
I sang.
She roared.
I fixed.
She tore.
We had a friendship.
No more.

I'M NOT SORRY

Go ahead and spin the record,
but I'm not gonna sing that sorry song you wrote for
me.
The melody sucks, and my ears don't like to hear it
much because it's all a fabrication.
You're creating lies and making a dime off my time, so
I'm not singing it, and no, I'm not sorry either.
That sad song says nothing about me and my nation,
how you picked it apart is pure degradation, so I don't
understand the fascination you've fantasized
about. You're not turning me out nor selling me down
stream for your dream off the sweat of my black back.

So spin the record, but you won't hear my beautiful
voice over the track.
I'd rather sing on the side of the streets, next to a
homeless man while he's tapping out my beat.
Vibrating my sound while underground might not be
so bad, even after you offered me all you claimed you
had, I still come out on top because your mountain of
money can't force me to drop my dignity.
I'll stick to scraping around for my pennies while
watching you burn inside, keep smirking while you
pretend that you have it all together but really can't
decide what you're going to do without me since I
refuse to sing your sorry song.

Now look who's dreams are gone.

VERSE

All that sitting on a track that you boast and brag
about, drag my name through the mud behind my
black back attack, but I still left you broken behind
closed doors, squirming around on all fours,
wallowing in all that green that you tried to give me,
but that *you* really need, if I sing that song.
Like I told you before, the melody sucks, and my ears
don't like to hear it much because the man who wrote
it was a liar, creating fabrications to make money off
of my dispensation, so I'm not singing it, and no, I'm
not sorry either.

I heard what you said because you said it like an old,
loud preacher, except there was no choir, when you
fired off
that I wouldn't amount to a hill of shame and no stars
would ever light up my name.
Said without you, I would be nothing, and if I didn't
sing that song, you tried to convince me that my life
would be gone but you made a drastic mistake.
My worth was something you could never cause me to
contemplate because why would I close my eyes to my
own demise behind a sad sack of dreams you touted
were for me, when in reality, those dreams were only
for your pocket...so I knocked it.

If you would have listened, I told you that the melody
sucks. It's a crime and an unlovely story, painted with
brushes and not fingertips, written with water and not
sand, scrubbed down with ice and not etched in skin
with the sun.

VERSE

The song is in shambles and made to ramble about
nothing, dishonest about my something.
So just spin the record, but you won't get my voice
over the track. I'd rather sing on the side of the dusty
streets than beg for my priceless soul back.

CORRUPT PRESIDENTS

Lock him up.
Seal the cage.
He dressed in a suit,
but like an animal he behaved.

Lock him up.
Toss the key.
He played that stock market,
stealing from the poor like me.

Lock him up.
Chain him down.
He broke every law,
hiding evidence underground.

Lock him up.
Make no escape.
He's not above the law.
His cell awaits.

LIFE SAVING LOVE

If I could take my love and fly away, I would.
When I feel the urge to drop him from the sky, I
wouldn't.
I fear that he would crumble without me.

If my love would crumble without me,
Then a naive girl would have to sweep up the mess,
With no idea that he can't be put back together.
I digress…

If he can't be put back together,
Then there is only one purpose for the sweep.
We will mourn for his life together and clutch his dust
as we sleep.

And when we both awaken to his ash,
I will steal the most important pieces of the stash.
His heart will be gone, flying in the sky with me
again…

Alas.

MY HAIR?

My hair is real, and
my teeth are pearly white.
My feet are wealthy, and
my melanin is tight.
My tongue flicks pure gold, and
my lips aren't small.
My wit is what I love
most of all.

My hair is real, and
you may not know it.
My hair is real, but
you swear I can't grow it.
My hair is mine,
coming from a long line.
My hair is fit,
the unbreakable kind.

My hair is real, and
my breath smells like rose.
My scent is fresh
on the way up your nose.
My legs are long, and
my arms are, too.
My brilliance is so perfect
that it only blesses you.

VERSE

But all you think about is my hair.

SWEET DREAMS YOU ARE

You are my precious jewel
worth more than diamonds and everything.
You are my streams of ponds
and oceans made of gold.
You are my unseen star,
my destiny to unfold.

You aren't my disappointment,
no matter what comes next,
because the love I hold for you
is simply too complex.

Whenever I say something
that you would rather not hear,
or think of something crazy that
somehow vibrates in your ear
remember that…

You are my secret dreams

worth more than diamonds
and everything,
and my love for you overrides
any disappointing things.

LOVE THOUGHT

It's important to love yourself before falling in love.
That way you don't spend your years with someone
who is in love with your self-hatred.

RACIST RATIONALE

With her black self…

She has black children
With a black man.
That forms a black family,
And they're married, too.

Her black children are smarter than mine.
I must admit, I get jealous from time to time.
Her black man even earns a good living, too.
They don't beg, steal or nickel and dime for their due.

They really are a black family,
And I'm so shocked they aren't depraved.
When they moved into my neighborhood,

VERSE

I just about died and went to my grave!

I would look out my window
And peep through the blinds.
It was all I could do to keep from crying
When her family behaved better than mine.

With her black self…

LOVE?

It's amazing how you love me,
caress me, and then suddenly,
take me in your arms
to sound my alarms
when you beat me.

It's so amazing.

It's so amazing how you love me,
while massaging my feet, and then momentarily,
scold me with your eyes and
slug me in my thighs
while hiding your fist
under the tablecloth.

It's so amazing.

It's so amazing how you love me
while spinning your web of Honey,

dripping her poisonous sauce on my heart
and humored as she rips it apart.

It's so amazing.

It's so amazing how you love me,
and it's crazy how I let you see
how hurt I live while you
walk about so happily.

It's so amazing.

It's so amazing how I loved you
and disregarded my truth
until I woke up and realized
I'd already murdered you.

It's so amazing … your kind of love.

REDUNDANCY

Ordinarily, I would look you from head to toe,
curse you with every language that I know,
and afterwards, continue on my way.

Ordinarily, I would, because you disrespect me so,
call you out your name and let you know that
the hottest part of hell is where you can go.

VERSE

I would ordinarily ball up my fists
and dream of beating you down like you did me last
night.
You caught me with my back turned, snuck me,
and then won the fight.

Ordinarily, I would have asked for round two
and wouldn't have spared a second hit,
but I'm so tired of fighting.
Today, I'm calling it quits.
I'm too old for this.

FACESHAWL

Hidden.
She's so shawled up,
even balled up
because her walls are up
after being knocked up
and mocked up,
so sad she even choked up,
so lost she even coked up,
thought she was washed up
'til one day she stood up,
wiped her mess up,
then got dressed up,
decided to confess up

to get freed up
so she could fix that crown up
to catch the blessings
that were on the way down.
Found.

WHEN I DIE, REMEMBER ME AS

Remember that funny joke that
rang laughter into your eyes,
allowing tears to drizzle down
like raindrops from the sky.

Recall that unheard melody that
was felt in your chest
that continues for many moons
without pausing for a rest.

When I die, I want you to remember
that circle of memories that,
since birth,
traces beyond three-hundred sixty degrees.

When I die, forget me dead,
but remember me as that rain,
recall me as that melody,
rewrite me as that circle.

VERSE

Enjoy me still.

Remember me as alive.

NOT YOU

I was always a divine dark
with a bright, shining light.

I was always so skinny
with tremendous fight.

I was always too smart
with a strange voice saying you can't.

I was always too caring
with a faint anger chant.

I was forever too wise
with an ignorance so brutal.

I was always too social
with a plan so futile.

I was always too dry
with a weep-soaked pillow.

I was always too careful
with room for error so little.

VERSE

When I look back on things,
I was always myself.

When I look back on life,
I'm glad I wasn't someone else.

CENTER STAGE

Place me on center stage
with my speckles sneaker shoes and gold parade.
Glance at the cloth falling over my legs
and the cut off drapery that supports my upper mades.

Place me smack dab in the middle so that everybody
can see
these thin threads that line my thighs and
that five inch wood standing me up so high.

Place me on top of the world
Butt naked without my pearls.
I still look good at my center stage.

Place me on center stage
when the wax of my age is no longer cold,
the lines of my body cover me like roads of gold
and the magnificence of God radiates through the
wrinkles in my skin.
Being old is not a sin.

VERSE

Place me smack dab in the middle so that everybody
can see
every strand of my gray hairs and the miracle of life
that covers me.

Place me on top of the world
Butt naked with these pearls.
I still look good at my center stage.

HE'S A JOKE

He's such a joke.
He doesn't even have to write the gags or
rehearse the jest.
He's the clown, and he's the best.

He holds himself high, trying to make others feel low.
He brandishes his knowledge, but his wisdom is slow.
He creates a facade, but when called on it, he breaks.
He believes he's a hero, but he's a sure flake.

He's such a joke.
He doesn't even have a paying crowd.
He's a clown, and he's the best around.

THE RECONCILIATION

We've been away for a while.
We didn't talk.
Mouths steadily distant,
Our bodies in a state of shock.

We've been away for a while.
Too much pain to climb.
The bed was empty, though
our bodies intertwined.

We've been away for a while.
Yes, it's been too long.
But now that we are back as one,
Let's make it last so very long.

PANDEMIC 2020

Death came down,
and we all had to hide in place,
shelter under the red bricks,
crawl underneath wooden sticks,
but somehow,

81

VERSE

it found us,
seeping in with the air we breathe,
laughing as it drained its disease,
strained its disease, about our heads,
thousands of us dissipated in dread,
but one day,
it all went away,
leaving the corpses to decay,
but the heartache to stay.

MIND BOGGLING

It's so mind boggling that
flowing through my body
is the power to overcome all adversity,
drain oceans of hatred,
and destroy miles of milestones
that draped like curtains around my neck,
and even yet,
I still have the capacity to snap back
when you throw shade at my seed,
an untouchable breed,
born with the stamina greater than one million
infantry,
womb-prepped with a gait that fifty stallion can't beat,
spirits so close to God that when our feet stomp
the stars shake,
and when our hands clap
the planets vibrate;

the heavens enjoy that sound of the real saints of God
whom He gave the faith-filled fortitude to walk on
water,
when the world wanted us to sink in dread,
but my ancestors hollered out "But Jesus said!"
because even though the white man tore it out,
they still sneaked and read,
refusing the partial of everything and dismissing the
sum of all zeroes,
we refuse to disengage for our heroes,
spitting fire that wounds like silver lead,
slaying evil angels and putting that witchcraft to bed
so it can wake up drenched in black sweat,
drowning in black tears while suffocating in death
defying black skin.
It's mind boggling how
we
still
win.

HOPE

If you swallow me whole,
vomit my silver lining,
and keep my gold,
drain my arteries,
narrow my life down,
clot my memories,
and keep my crown,

limit my choices, and
select what I'm fed,
I might dread,
but dim my vision,
and I'd rather be dead.

GIRL

Fat girl,
stop calling that skinny girl a wack girl.
Quit shading on her shine,
and treading her thin lines
like God drew her as an offensive motif,
raking harsh pain across her frame
like she's a dried up leaf.

Skinny girl,
stop calling that fat girl a wack girl,
striking her make with belittling buckets of water,
dragging her frame from one dusty corner to another
like she deserves no better fate.

Just wait.

VERSE

Wack girl,
the one who looks down on any other girl,
the one who reflects her mess onto others
so they can stress,
spreading spiteful decay like poisoned butter on toast,
spending hours admiring her for your next roast.
Your pen ain't lit,
and your words ain't flame.
If you're gonna call another girl anything,
call her by her name.

SPIT

Spit on me, and I bloom.

Don't let the sun shine on me too soon.
Let the air freeze over my wounds.
Allow the mighty birds to come fumble through my
tomb.
Order the sky to close its large eyes from my presence.
Request the moisture to vanish from my essence.

Spit on me, and I bloom.

Don't let the savage prance my way,
or the beast gallop near with majestic hooves.
Let the wind blow the blood from my far reaching
roots

and the mud suffocate my lacerated limbs.
Call the government of ants to mound upon my
nostrils
and the pillars of cacti to walk across my back.
Because no matter the attack,

Spit on me, and I bloom.

SOMEDAY, SOON WE GO

Someday, Soon will come from the heavens,
part the clouds like the Red Sea,
fire the land like Gomorrah and Sodom,
bruise the fame and uplift the lame,
drain the blood of the earth for miles like the Nile,
set the sun back because it thought itself far too
mighty
as the trumpets take their rightful places
against the dreary drums, and the rocks begin to hum,
sway side to side, dropping their pride,
because the praise dancers lost their legs,
fallen to the ground on bended knee,
so amazed at Who they see.

Someday, Soon will come strike the ground,
forbidding the earth to quake,

VERSE

but will shake the dirt from the dead prophets,
unlocking the pointless prisons that bound a multitude
of truths that could have salted the earth with its
healing tonic,
but the world didn't want it, so it used its own logic,
burying the familiar flavors that once saturated the
oceans, valleys and stones,
leaving the most celebrated creation lost and all alone.

Someday, Soon will ride the clouds,
and shut all this down.
He will send to gather, no matter where His are
scattered,
in the ashes of molten lava to the flesh basined bottom
of
the shadowed sea,
through the thick diamond mines
that dropped boulders atop forgotten minds
to the deserts of camouflage that hid centuries
of mysteries and miseries to level the pyramids that
concealed His treasures.
He will brandish secrets of the earth and finally cease
the weather.

Someday, Soon will come,
and we will go.
This old world we will no longer
yearn for, flesh that we will no longer
burn for.
And when everything is empty and all
leveled to dust, there will be another.
It won't remember us.

VERSE

There won't be any flashbacks.
There will be nothing old.
We will live with Him as He lives with us.
We will marvel at His throne.

PACE MAKER

Calm down, child, calm down.
Set your peace in the right place
so your heart can maintain its pace,
so you can grow strong though
trapped in this world of hate.

Calm down, child, calm down.
Roll the hum like grandma did
when she shielded her kids,
beyond the trees where black men hung,
so she could go and load her gun.

Calm down, child, calm down.
There is no cause for flutter.
There is no reason to mutter,
just stand behind grandma as she
goes to fight for her brother.

Calm down, child, calm down.
Grandma always comes from the back
to help Grandpa with the attack
to pick up the slack.

VERSE

Calm down, child, calm down.
There's no need to shriek,
no need to cry or frown.
One day you must also learn
how to take those lynchmen down.

Breathe.

EMOJI

I'm not an emoji.
I'm not a dot with a caricatured face
with fake pain
or cartoon names
with made-up memories
or digital tears
with red-colored rage
or sky-blue fears.

I'm not an emoji.
I'm not folded strands of caricatured hands
with empty touch
or unfounded prayer
with wasted worship
or motionless waves
with two dimensional fists
or silent praise.

VERSE

I'm not an emoji.
I'm as real as real can get
with agonizing pain
and an identifying name
with vivacious memories
and indestructible rage
with solemn tears
and conquered fears.

I'm not an emoji.
I'm so lit, I'm on fire
with lightening in my palms
and a burn in my tips
with thunder in my praise
and broken ground in my worship
with winding wrists for my waves
and an abounding spirit that forgave.

I'm not an emoji.
My face is really surprised
with a gap-toothed smile
and an afro-covered dome
with a mind of my own
and skin that refuses a wrinkle
with a black elasticity that helps me bounce back.

I'm not an emoji.
It's a wonder most don't know.
Don't put me in a tiny circle or rundown yellow box.
The world needs to know.
I'm all I got.

SOUND OFF

Let my people go,
or we will take our freedoms fo'sho.
Let my people walk.
We don't need to talk.
We've listened and paid attention
for four hundred plus years,
but the conversation was lopsided,
so we shifted that chat and then decided.

America lied.
Wipe out your eyes.

It had my blackness in chains.
It had your whiteness deranged.
It has my blackness defamed.
It has your whiteness shamed.
It had us on two different sides of
the tracks.

When Blacks move in, white bags are packed.
When white bags get packed, they head for the high
hills.
When Blacks get settled, more troubles begin.
A walk down the street could get Blacks accused.
A jog down the road could get their neck bruised.

VERSE

When Blacks spoke, it went over America's head.
When Blacks danced, silence was what America said.
When Blacks tired, America reckoned we were dead.
When Blacks got angry, we tore America to shreds.

This is still my America,
But will it ever listen to what we said?

8

Count.
Don't stop until you reach that figure.
In that time, a black man may die from a cop's
trigger finger, pulling back on the metal
as you say the number six,
Not the same as common crime,
like gang on gang because
they speak that street slang
and live by their own creed,
unlike cops who are paid oath takers
swearing to uphold the highest deeds.

Count.
Don't stop until you reach that figure.
In that time, my black sister may die from white
silence,
her life cut short because they refused to be defiant

but chose to remain violent,
her seed murdered because they didn't want to bend.
Thought it more important to keep up with the racist
trend.

Count.
I need to shout but can't get it out.
I need to get free but can't move about.
I need to inhale but being pressed by knees.
I need to live but I can't breathe.

COUNTERFEIT

Have a seat.
Listen to this counterfeit beat.
Hear the way this land was founded,
broken and bruised bones,
women raped and hounded,
people shipped over the deep dark seas,
thrown into the dirt without even a please,
unlicensed sounds, dances and inventions,
stolen babies, promises and stifled premonitions.

Freedom's flag flew over
black bodies being ripped apart,
blood drizzled, poured and splattered over everything

else that mattered,
snaked all the power from the powerful
and all the blessings from the blessed,
stood tall atop mountains of stolen tapestries
with such ease,
using fresh bones of Black people to cover their
inhumane disease.

It's all counterfeit. Chile, please.
Rushing to arrest the black poor for doing
what founding fathers did,
hustling to kill the start of a future that gives
credit where they left it to die,
hoping it had no more life to cry.
But still black tears cry out for justice,
cry out against the beast,
cry out against the lies,
cry out all across the streets,
cry out against this counterfeit,
bringing hope to the future
and justice to the deceased.

SALT

sprinkle it.
it doesn't take much.
it moves a burdening mood
and lightens a heavy weight.

its strength is so magnificent that
it lifts the entire plate.

WHEN I'M UP

When I am up,
I won't forget when I was down,
toenails soiled over in dirt
and head hung low to the ground,
singing lullabies to the grass so it
cushions my sore back with massages each night
while in the day, I prayed,
God let it rain to wash all my filth away.

When I am down,
I won't forget when I was up,
toenails polished in the poshest of colors,
and chin scrapping the dew from one side of the sky
to the other,
singing aloud to the dancing dandelions that
drink the water from lush soil
while I praised God for His rain which left me
no shame as it still washed all my filth away.

VERSE

SLOW RIVER

I've sat here watching this same river,
this same river flowing one way down,
spreading its slanderous stories from town to town.

I've sat here washing in this same river,
this same river flowing one way down,
spreading its terror from town to town.

I've sat here listening to this same river,
this same river flowing one way down,
celebrating its lynchings from town to town.

I've sat here escaping this same river,
this same river flowing one way down,
spreading its hatred from town to town.

Today, I walked into this same river,
this same river flowing one way down.
I pushed against this same river,
but it was too weak to make me drown.

I AM

Even if I'm deaf and blind,
you'll still hear and see me shine.

VERSE

Even if my limbs won't run and arms won't wave,
you will witness the marathons I win and
the paths I pave.

Even if my parents are gone and I'm on this earth all
alone,
you will watch my wonders and see me leave a legacy
of my own.

Even if I have no money, scraping by on molded
bread,
you will still see me bless my Lord Jesus, keep
my faith, not fear, instead.

Even if I fail to exist and die deep into my sleep,
I'll still be all I am, my memory, for you to keep.

PEACE

Tell me about that peace I've never had,
the kind that moves in silence,
creeps up on you like stillness
and partakes in your soul
like a temptation
or the kind that leaves a person in awe,
yeah, like that peace from Yah.

The only type of peace I know
comes from cries in the middle of the night

or screams from gunshots in fright
and the mood that puts fists through concrete,
the dead hollering from beneath the streets
for somebody…anybody... to break them out.
That's the peace I know about.

Even though I know heaven is wide awake
and the earth quakes every time a heart breaks,
and even though I know the way God's mercy
falls down in the form like dew,
I still need to hear you.
I still need to hear from you all,
though all your noise is foul,
and the totality of visual pain and abnormalities
are lodged in brutalities,
I still need to hear you because it's something about
that loud heartbeat that allows me to rest.
I can hear it thumping when peace is at its best,
but when the noise and the shouting stops,
I am traumatized and lost.

Having rolled around in its muddiness
since the first time the air tossed me around,
through it, my feet carried me, even on shaky ground.
My nose soon steered me away from foul places,
and then my eyes guided me to another dance
that made just as much noise as the one
I was birthed into by chance.

But when I walked into that crowd of crooked backed,
hollerin' Black people who were swingin' and
shoutin',

their heads so far back like they were drinking sweet
honey
from the high trees,
their mouths so wide, their vocal chords collided,
making the sound come out as one
to One Whom they couldn't see,
collapsing on bended knee,
scraping grass with their skin, it was then.

That other peace I'd never known, caught me by
surprise,
shoved me into the crowd of angels that lifted me high,
as I soared above all the noise,
God let me look down so I could understand that peace
that seemed to run from me, or me from it,
so by the time He let me back to the land,
He never let go of my hand,
making my claps turn to praise
and my stomps put the devil in a daze.
It was that noise, that Holy noise that became my
peace.
No longer lost.
The other noise ceased.

Peace.

CONQUEROR

Life,

don't give me death,
for if you give me death,
I will conquer every weed,
rip every vile root and rotten seed,
pluck the brittle branches that
already broke under the pressure.
I will kill death because
my life has no measure.

Life,
don't leave me for dead,
for if you leave me for dead,
You will witness the greatest fight of all days.
I will toil and sweat,
even put my fist through the blazing sun,
come back and burn death to ash,
and won't stop until I'm done.

Life,
don't show me my end,
for if you show me my end,
I will discard every page of that script,
reverse the speech and combat the crypt.
I will dig the hole deep and strangle the trap,
spit on death's grave, and take my life back.

DADDY DEAREST

VERSE

Daddy Dearest,
Mommy's gone.
She went somewhere,
and she won't come home.

Daddy Dearest,
why do you sit there,
just sit there and stare?
Mommy woulda' said,
"Get up! Work is out there!"

Daddy Dearest,
what's wrong?
And what's taking Mommy so long?
I done went outside, played and back,
Mommy's still not home.

Daddy Dearest,
Did you do something bad?
The police are outside the door.
Am I gonna be sad?

Daddy Dearest,
you just keep staring,
and I'll unlock the door.
I'll do like you taught me…
lay down and put my hands
out and on the floor.

Daddy Dearest,
the front door is open,
and I'm doing as you said.

VERSE

Please, put the gun down now,
don't shoot yourself in the head!

Daddy Dearest,
wake up!
Wake up, Daddy, please!
Somebody get my momma!
"Little girl, put that gun down.
Freeze!"

Daddy Dearest,
I'm scared.
They shot me in my belly.
Daddy, wake up.
Am I gonna die?
I'm not ready.

VERSE

Write it down.
Chew it up.
Spit it out.

Leave it there.
Cover it.
Let it sprout.

Water it.

VERSE

Nurture it.
Watch it grow.

Love it.
Speak it.
Let the world know.

BLACK CHILD

Dear black child,
stay strong and stay proud.
Jesus loves you, just how you are.
God makes you shine far brighter
than every star.

Dear black child,
listen to no lies.
The heavens marvel at your style.
The angels wish they had your
physique.
You're just that unique.

Dear black child,
Stand and fear no man.
Create craters with your gait
and split the earth with your rage.
You weren't born to be caged.

Dear black child,

you're never on your own.
Hover over the hills and
vanish beneath the valleys.
In your fight to stay alive,
even the rocks pray toward
your vitality.

Dear black child,
Live like life needs your fire.
Share your skin like salt in sands.
Be earth's desire.
Stand in God's plan.

REVOLUTION

Prepare for the revolution?
It's already televised.
You've been asleep on the couch.
When you wake up,
don't be surprised.
You missed the war that's gone on
for over four hundred long years,
the killing of black babies
year after year,
the rape of black families
so the white ones could thrive,
but it cost us black folks our
precious short lives.

VERSE

Prepare for the revolution?
Black folks have been fighting
since before day one,
our fists against the whips
and our veins against the ropes,
our bellies against the barrels,
and knives against our throats.
Forced onto a ship,
chained up in my own motherland
passed from black hand to white hand,
the whole thing was planned.

Prepare for the revolution?
Let me tell you the entire truth.
Black folks were born into the fight,
we always raise the roof.
We always bear the scars,
and we'll always wear the crown,
whether at the bottom or at the top,
the revolution is going down.

FIGHT

He held hands with his twin sister.
They got on the swings.
They time warped into the future
to see what it would bring.
They time warped into the former

to see what was long gone.
Sadly, they found they had to keep
swinging on.

He gripped the chains with his twin sister.
They swung harder on the swings.
They time warped into the future
to see what it would bring.
They time warped into the former
to see what was gone.
Assured, they found they had to keep
swinging on.

He leaped from the swings with his twin sister.
Both let loose from the chains.
They time warped into the future
to see what they had gained.
They time warped so far up
that they left the present behind.
Rewarded, they enjoyed swinging
finally shouting, this land is mine.

HER LIFE

The only time one would see her teeth
was when she would eat.
She could carve a deep-fried drumstick

and not leave a bit of meat.
She could break the same bone
and suck the marrow clean.
She would pick her teeth with a thin stick
and rinse her mouth in between.

The only time one would see her rest
was when she would sleep.
She would close her brown eyes
and never make a peep.
She would move not a muscle
and shuffle not an inch.
She would reach for her gun
if any sound made her flinch.

The only time one would see her mourn
was when she would weep.
She would rock from side to side,
mumbling about the sow and the reap.
She would hum so silently
at the pain she must forgive.
She would fight her memories
of the heartaches she must relive.

I'M SO DONE

Chile, I'm so done.
I can't wait to get outche'.

VERSE

Been sittin' 'round,
smokin' bud,
turnin' up,
and shootin' guns.

Chile, I'm so fed up.
I can't wait to leave this place.
Been dreamin' of leavin'
every night,
passin' the time,
and startin' fights.

Chile, I'm ret' to be gone.
I can't wait to bounce.
Been tastin' my next forty
and spittin' my next gin,
I gotta stop this though,
'lesson I be stuck right here again.

THE UPTICK

It's never enough.
A small increase toward the decrease of
injustice.

It's never enough.
A tiny kick in the right direction
only to later get a bad deflection.

VERSE

It's never enough.
A song with the right words
but the wrong tune,
A dream with the right vision
but forgotten too soon.
A life with the right material,
but the wrong foundation.
A history with superior pain,
but no road for its annihilation.

It's never enough.
Justice grown for some
but not for all.
A march atop the White House,
but it doesn't hear our call.

ENSLAVED CRIES:SHORT WEEPS

The cries of the enslaved,
I can still hear beneath the rotten dirt
in the graves.
When I sleep at night,
they sound off in my ears.
When I walk in the day,
they won't lead me astray.

The cries of the enslaved,

I can still hear them beneath the bloody waters
in the graves.
When I swim in the seas,
the water boils my skin.
When I run on the beach,
the salt burns me within.

The cries of the enslaved,
I can still hear them in my heart's pounds.
They will weep harder and harder,
until true freedom sounds.

ENSLAVED CRIES: LONG WAILS

Have you ever wondered what happened to the cries of
the enslaved, though the enslaved are gone buried deep
somewhere in unmarked graves?

Have you ever considered them trapped inside the
womb, a pain so deep that it couldn't be contained
inside a tomb,
a pain so alive that it crept into the path of the
descended, decades into centuries couldn't mend it.

Have you ever considered the cries of the enslaved,

how God adopted baby after baby when their fathers
were slain
and the mothers laid in the blood, drowning their own
bodies in an anguish they couldn't reveal, a pain that
never healed?

Have you ever thought about where all that pain went
because energy doesn't disappear nor is it spent?
The cries of those in bondage, shackled in hatred and
greed,
prayed the prayer of freedom, and the song rang out in
their seed.

Have you ever pondered over the seed that was left,
how they were designed from the deserted and
nourished of the dream, overlooked by the cherished
and built from screams,
how they tremble at nothing and they dive on your ass,
how they march until their feet go numb for a justice
that will last?

Have you ever thought about the enslaved and how
they nourished food out of their tears, when the rain
stopped coming, the salt water from their eyes grew
crops year after year?

Have you ever looked inside the eyes of their young
and spotted a tribe of their forefathers marching at
heaven's gates, their holy noise so loud until the
firmament breaks?

Then it all goes silent as Jesus comes through because
God promised his children He would come to the
rescue.

Have you ever considered the cries of the enslaved,
how they were never buried but live on beyond the
grave?
Have you, oh have you, ever marveled at how their
wails remain?

THE GREAT TAP OUT

She fixin'ta tap out, they laughed.
She couldn't stack up to her fake task.

She called the cops,
said she was scared,
cops got there,
she like to fall out dead.
Nobody was holdin' her.
No one was in her face.
The black man that she screamed about
even stood in place.

He pointed at her.
She pointed at him.
We held up our phones,
and her ugly face fell grim.
The cop started talkin'.

VERSE

She tried to block him out.
She started talkin' louder.
We all started to shout.

We put her face on the gram
so everyone could see her flinch.
She tapped out.
We didn't harm her one inch.

MY DREADS

My dreads are made for my head,
not made for you to pick, yank or tug,
rule out, deride, plus I'm not a thug.

These are my dreads,
my shelter from the cold,
when the world wants me less bold-
placing me in a shell,
telling me to move neither here nor there,
castigating my methods and upbraiding my
upbringing,
chiding my thoughts and lambasting my singing.

These are my dreads,
and they are made for my kind,
who deliver praise back to Yah
in faithfulness by design,

VERSE

who take up the vow to reign
under He Who is Divine,
to stand strong as my locs
stroll down my back, destined to intertwine.

My dreads are how I dress.
Your stringy clothes on me are a mess.
I prefer drapes in heaven-mades,
kinky crevices through my scalp,
layering across my shoulders,
slicing the thick winds as I whip my hair back.

These are my principles,
the dreads I live by each day,
keepsakes of my memories,
highlights of my reflections,
engraved to teach my children
everlasting lessons.

My dreads you secretly admire,
oh how they burn you like fire,
and make you second guess
how they would blend on your ends,
but the handsomeness of their tones
doesn't quite work with your own.

These locs are my rhythmical beats.
My dreads strum the city streets.
They suppress the howling horns
that wage war against my silky thorns.
They stick you and prick you
because it's a mystic to you,

how they guide my stride
and comfort me when I lay,
their beauty on full display.

My dreads.
They're made for my head,
not made for you to pick, yank or tug,
rule out or deride.
They deserve to be seen.
My dreads I won't hide.

JUST FINE

I'm not like you,
and that's just fine.

If you don't care for me,
walk another line.

If you can't stand me,
and around me you won't tread,
keep that to yourself.
Your negative thoughts
won't clog my head.

If you need to spray me with venom
and hope it penetrates my skin,
dominates my dreams and

changes me from within,
understand that I'm more complex
than what you could ever know.
Your venom isn't lethal to me.
In time, your wounds will show.

I'm not like you,
and that's just fine.

If you don't care for me,
just walk another line.
Draw your own path,
and stop treading on mine.

PERFECT BLACK MAMA

Black Mama, Black Mama,
there was nothing perfect around you.
You came up under racism and stuff,
learned from broken books,
cooked from crooked pans,
bathed in freezing water
in the middle of winter's snow,
even gave me your sheets when we
were put out the doe'.

116

VERSE

Black Mama, Black Mama,
there was nothing perfect around you.
You had a little bit of dimes
while everyone else had dollars,
scrubbed my garments with suds
even when there was no soap,
found fabric you could sew
so they wouldn't see my holey clothes
no mo'.

Black Mama, Black Mama,
there was nothing perfect about you.
You cried in the night
and still smiled in the day,
cooked a hot meal,
even on depressed days.
We didn't know everything was sad and such,
but you still made time to feed and teach us.

Black Mama, Black Mama,
There was nothing imperfect about you, no.
We still love you so much, Black Mama.
We can't stand to see you go,
but when you get to heaven,
and march around your new place,
look down at all us imperfect children,
and ask the Lord to give us His grace.

RELEASE

Am I allowed to be angry at you, dear Africa?
Am I allowed to get it off my chest?
Am I allowed to scream at the top of my lungs
and you still lay out a blanket for me to rest?

Am I allowed to be angry at you, Europe?
Am I allowed…oh yes I am.
Am I allowed to topple the statues you love
like you tore apart my black lands?

Am I allowed to forgive you, dear Africa?
Am I allowed to set my soul free?
Am I allowed to reach beyond the pain and sorrow,
and rebuke the evils mankind placed on me?

Am I allowed to forgive you, Europe?
Am I allowed to open my arms?
Am I allowed to use all the strength in me,
and pay you any regard?

Am I allowed to cry a river?
Am I allowed to weep a many seas?
Am I allowed to break ten thousand monuments
without any of you judging me?

KIN

I love all my kin.
I love them now, and I loved them back then.
We didn't come up the same,
and we didn't always sing the same tune.
Life is too short for hatred,
no matter the color because
we'll all be the same color dead real soon.

MISUNDERSTOOD

Denied because of her beauty.
Singled out because of her words.
Her vocals barely run vain,
but her voice strains, clearly unheard.

Asking her why she's loud,
questioning why she snaps,
figuring she has an attitude,
forgetting she's been under attack.

Denied because of his strength.
Singled out because of his charm.
His hustle never runs weak,

119

and his forethought never unarmed.

Asking him why he's so loud,
questioning why he flares,
figuring he has a problem,
forgetting injustice pushed him there.

EVIL HAS NO COLOR

Evil has no color.
It's like crystal clear glass
broken on the sharp edges of another,
like electricity in a cord
that kills with a shock,
like poison in the air
that makes hearts stop.
Evil has no color.
It's like tears in a dream
and moisture above the sea,
like riches of diamonds
that choke so deceptively.

Evil has no color.
It's like hunger in the night,
and like pain in the day,
like suffering in mourning
and rage at play.

Evil has no color.

VERSE

It's like lies on the street,
and disobedience on a bridge,
like dishonor on the tongue
and rifts on a smooth ridge.

Evil has no color.
It's like demons in the deals
and the destruction of depth,
like murders in the heart
until there's nobody left.

YOUTH

When I was a child,
we used to clap,
fold our bodies back,
haul off and slap
our hands together
in such sync,
our motions revealed
something so deep.

When I was a child,
we used to dance,
catapult our bodies,
set onlookers in a trance,
on the way back down
hands still in the sky,

land on the ground
with taps that burn our thighs.

When I was a child,
we used to sing,
stand in a group
our souls to cling,
open our mouths
to belt it out,
sing, stand and stare
then clap it out.

When I was a child,
we used to clap,
fold our bodies back
haul off and slap
our hands together
in such joy,
didn't rush to be adults,
just girls and boys.

NOT SPOON-FED

She was fed with a fork. Never could get her soup
from the bowl, and there were no straws to hold the
nutrients inside while she tried to suck it all up.

VERSE

This was her life, hoping to climb, but the trees never had limbs, mountains were too smooth, and even when she went to the beach, the waters were far too dry.
 Starfish died.
Things were so hard for her at times that the good life would have been something she would have never denied.

She would cry sometimes because her loose change never made a dollar, and there were times that the streets failed to make a strong delivery to ease her monetary misery.
Her feet could walk, and she was thankful, but they remained scorched because her dainty sandals were hand-me-overs, being passed from one person to another, with holes in the soles.

People were so cold, her torn winter coat wasn't enough protection from their scolds. It was the icy weather that kept her warm, made her remember that it was just a seasonal storm that would pass, while the hatred battered her over-moisturized yet still far too dry skin, not to mention her eyes.
She would blame the freezing wind on her tears to camouflage her cries.

She ate with a fork. Never could get her soup from the bowl, and there were never any straws to hold the nutrients inside so she could try to suck it down.
She didn't want to appear like a glutton at the table full of strangers who could use their utensils to sop their food out.

VERSE

She opted to wait on their escape, when they would all
leave the room, to turn her bowl of water back down
her throat...

because she didn't have a spoon.

PITY ANN FOOL

She thought he loved her.
He would send her flowers and call her every hour,
and in the minutes before the next, she would flex...tell
everyone how good he tended to be, make them sit and
barely listen to her long, love story because she would
tell it every time she felt the need to hide the shame of
the other woman who called his name.

She had to dress him up.
He would send the other woman love poetry and call
her every minute, and in the seconds before the next,
she would still falsely flex...talk about how he made
her light up, strike a match and send her heart into
flames, but those flames kept her trapped between the
doors of rage and a bullet between his brain.

She thought he loved her.
He would stumble inside the house in the middle of
the dark morning, fall into her comfort zone and
disturb her aching bones with more bruises than she
cared to count. She just laid there with no concept of

how to make it end, but she knew the very next bright
day, she would flex again, just so everyone could see
just how wonderful a relationship she was in.

She tried to kill him.
He would bring her flowers and call her every hour,
and in the minutes before the next, she stopped the
routine and finally truly flexed...placed one round that
she'd found at the back of some smooth metal, backed
away and made him think before she blew his evil
threats directly into that stainless steel kitchen sink.

She went down in cuffs.
He went down with his neck cocked and his eyes
rolled back into his head. She stared at his lifeless
mouth, no longer able to do what he boastfully
said. She smiled as they gathered her callous attitude
from the blood-stained floor, describing her actions as
crazy and even cruel, but when they requested her
name, she flexed once more and replied...

My name is Mrs. Pity Ann Fool.

From that time on, people pitied her because they'd
already seen through her lies, that all the things in her
love life weren't so grand, but just fairy tales and
lullabies. A fool is what some others started to call her,
said she was a sure heap of mess, hanging around a
man who beat her and cheat her, but then there were
some who confessed, gave her much props because
she finally got the drop on that man.
So they continued to respect her as little Mrs. Ann.

HER NAME WAS POOR

Her name was Poor.

Even though she had a wide smile with a wealth of winding hair that slid across the marble floors beneath her high back, posh chair while her toes practiced their tips and her palms massaged the gravel, she was adored from The Bottoms because she forced herself so high up that the necks of those who sought after her became broken at their joints as they strained to gain her gait from point to point, from coming and going, her presence was pushed, and when she stared down onto the beautiful city, she kept her face of stone because what made her a beauty was long gone.

The people from The Bottoms loved her. They always called for her to come back down, to help them live their lives and splash in the muddy puddles on the grimy ground because they remember what they used to call her while they were also proud of where she'd been which is why all night long they would dance and sometimes even sing, banging the bricks of the high rise under the brightly black sky until she finally stood out onto the barren balcony and dropped down from the sun...

Her wings stopped working, and Poor Baby was done.

VERSE

UNLIKEABLE

There are no two ways to spell it. I'm what you call
unlikeable because I speak my mind all the time, and
whenever I try and hold it back, it comes to the roof of
my mouth and then to the tip of my tongue, freedom
breaks the chains of my internal structure, and it
comes pouring out, one word after another. They sit
there and listen to my distressing words, be they the
truth or not lying down enough. That's all they've got
to hear whenever I draw near, making me so
unlikeable.

I've tried to edit my posture, sit with my back up
straight and shorten my walk, you know, hide my
stride as if it won't be visualized and then brutalized.
I've attempted to do this over and over again, but then
I would start to bend and my walk wouldn't look so
presentable to the naked eyes that watch me and how I
go against the grain. Dang...at least I tried, but I can
no longer remain hidden, concerned about being
disliked or despised. What is inside must always pour
out into bowls.

I suppose that's why the good Lord made us with
holes. I don't know, maybe I'm just too bold. How

dare I tell you when you're dead wrong or when I speak up against the injustices on the streets or inside your own office, hiding your crimes behind a suit doesn't mean you can call me a brute. At least I can say that my money isn't all funny, and myself, I don't have to conceal just to make a transaction that leaves whole neighborhoods packing but millions of extra dollars in my pocket. You walk around like an adjustable rate, not fixed on anything except your pockets and how to keep your lies straight. You're double-minded as hell, yeah, hell is like that, too, functioning just like Satan trying to get people to do what you want them to do, so you can strip their lives from beneath them, making crooked laws so you can deplete them.

I see your ways, and I know you see mine which is why you have called me ignorant, stupid and just plain black from time to time, like that last adjective is so bad. You mad? Wait a minute, I'm sorry, I just put you in a rage as a result of the truth uncaged, but this is what the truth in freedom sounds like, walks like and talks like, moves like and grooves like, commands like and stands like. But that's exactly why it's like...

Unlikeable.

HUNGRY SPIRITS DIE

Hungry spirits die.
Can't meet the birds in the sky.
No need to moan and cry
because you fed yourself a lie.
You ate everything from the pig's feet to the pork chops,
even nasty canned yams.
You even sopped your biscuits up
with Grandma's favorite jam.
But you forgot to eat one thing,
so it shouldn't come as a surprise
that if you don't eat God's Word,
your spirit will starve to death and die.

HELLO, AFRICA

to you, i say hello.

i never got the chance to say good-bye.
i bring a message in my eyes
from centuries ago,
back to families i do not know
who one day awoke to desperate cries
when slave traders came to ruin their lives,
kill their kin and drain their souls,
induce severe pains for the young and old,
create so much confusion it left all in despair,
so much anguish it dominated the air.

VERSE

to you, africa, i send a message from
your stolen ones, the sold ones,
the ones who digested agony,
the ones whose mothers from the Land wailed
desperately
because the distance from their children was too brutal
but they still had so much to fight through over there,
so much it seems that we all got lost in the shuffle,
creating new worlds in our own small bubbles
so that we could cope with the loss
that came at a terrible cost.

to you, i tell you God has a plan
and He won't let mankind's evil stand
so don't remain confused,
mothers who still weep in the graves
for their children who never remained.
We lived.
God kept his eyes on us, His prize on us,
though we were slaughtered and bruised,
enslaved and used,
He raised up a generation of descendants who haven't
forgotten,
about the ships they were brought in and bought in.
yes, to the victimized families of africa,
we still fight for our kin.
that was a message from our ancestors
until we meet again.

to you, i say hello.

VERSE

SPEAK ON IT

Damage control?
What did I break?
Tell me what I wrote so bad
that got you in this state.
Tell me what I wrote
that burned a hole through
your heart,
why you're so offended.
My language won't be amended
or made to help you understand,
drag you through explanations,
or lessen my grand stance.
My cipher is so gentle,
but hits with a solid punch,
offending liars
because the truth
weighs 'em down too much.
It comforts the straight forward,
soothing their screams,
letting it all out
makes honest hearts gleam.
Damage control?
What did I break?
How you feel doesn't matter
when too many lives are at stake.

VERSE

THE END

Thank you for reading VERSE. If you enjoyed it,
please leave a review.

Visit RoyaltyinBlack.com and ReadToFreedom.com
for T-Shirts and merchandise.
Visit BlackEntrepreneurHistory.com for the many
Black Entrepreneurs in History and their outstanding
contributions to all our lives.

Also, choose from the following list of books to enjoy
from AkirimPress.com authors Mirika Mayo
Cornelius, Rod Cornelius, and Cyan Deane.

VERSE

Historical Fiction
CURSE THE COTTON
THE SECRET NOVEL COLLECTION
THE DAY I MET FREEDOM
DISGUISED BY A RAGING SMILE
UGLY
GRANDMA'S GUN

Horror/Suspense
I THOUGHT I WAS ALONE TRILOGY
INSIDE THE GATES OF DOONS
THE TRUSTED

Urban
I WILL DO ANYTHING FOR HER
MOST WANTED FELON
COLD BLOODED GOONS
THE GABRIEL'S TRAILS MURDERS SINS &
DECPETION BOX SET
HE BEATS ME
WHATEVER IT TAKES
LOVE, LIES & LIPSTICK
THE BEST KEPT SECRETS
WHEN IT COMES AROUND

Dystopian
EXECUTION'S KARMA

Christian Thriller
AN EVIL WAS BORN

VERSE

Poetry
GHETTO EYES
VERSE

Noir
FIRST DEGREE SINS
DEAD MAN'S MAYHEM

Romance
SINGLE AGAIN
AIN'T QUITE WHAT I THOUGHT!
AIN'T QUITE WHAT I THOUGHT 2!
DIGGIN' GOLD

www.ingramcontent.com/pod-product-compliance
Lightning Source LLC
LaVergne TN
LVHW021350080426
835508LV00020B/2202